Twelve Step Guide to Writing A Theme-base Research Paper (Montgomery Bus Boycott of 1955)

by

Ramona L. Hyman, PhD

Copyright 2013 by Ramona L. Hyman
TXu 1-878-856

Special thanks for your support:
Cecily Daly
AleahHyman-Faulkner
Nicole Peeler
Rashida Pryce
Kasha Robinson
Patricia Wilson

Table of Contents

Letter to Instructor-friends

Greetings,

I hope you are ready to guide your students through an exciting research-writing journey: the theme-base research paper.

The theme-base research paper is one in which the student develops and writes the research paper using a general subject area. In this workbook, I have used the Montgomery Bus Boycott as the subject. Each student would choose a topic that is associated with this subject. An example is provided on the section entitled "Choose A Topic."

Guiding students through the research process employing a general theme is a meaningful and intellectually engaging assignment. The theme-base research paper also helps students to understand how many topics can be generated from one subject area.

Instructor-friends, the theme base research project encourages collaborative learning. I encourage you to have your students develop a mini conference on the subject. Each student would share the findings from his/her research. Instructions and suggestions for the mini conference are provided in the appendix of this workbook.

The example used in this workbook is the Montgomery Bus Boycott of 1955. I chose the Montgomery Bus Boycott of 1955 as a theme because I yearn for students to experience this important historical event. I want them to know the folks who, metaphorically speaking, stretched their imaginations up to the sky as they dreamed of equality in America. I want them to know of the men and women who walked 381 days in a place called Montgomery, Alabama so that all people could be treated equally on city buses. Finally, I hope students garner life lessons from the Montgomery Bus Boycott of 1955 story.

Note: In the resource section of the workbook, I have provided two other sample subject areas with topics.

Cheers,

Dr. Hyman

Letter to Students

Greetings Students,

For the next few weeks, you will be taking a twelve-step journey through the research paper writing process. You will develop a theme-base research paper. I have chosen as my theme base subject the Montgomery Bus Boycott of 1955. Your instructor may choose another subject.

Now just what is research writing?

Research writing, sometimes called writing with sources, provides one with the opportunity to delve into a variety of references on a specific topic. A theme-base research paper is one in which all of the papers will be on one subject. More information about the theme base research paper is on pages that follow.

Sources that you may use for your research project, moreover, may come from print as well as non-print materials such as books, newspaper articles, magazine articles, internet materials, movies, artifacts, museum presentations, interviews, and oral presentations.

This workbook is a 12 step sequential plan for developing the research paper.
It is easy to follow, so don't stress.

Finally, at the end of this journey, I hope you will have a research paper conference. I hope you will get an opportunity to share your research paper with your classmates.

Enjoy the journey!

Cheers,

Dr. Hyman

Step One:
Choose a Topic

This workbook provides steps to developing a theme base research project. This means that the instructor provides the students with a subject and the students can choose a topic from the subject.

Example One
Thematic subject: Montgomery Bus Boycott of 1955

Possible Topics:

1. Women's Participation in the Montgomery Bus Boycott
2. Dr. Martin Luther King, Jr.'s Contribution to the Montgomery Bus Boycott
3. Rosa Parks: The Protagonist of the Montgomery Bus Boycott
4. Browder V Gayle: The Court Case That Changed a Nation

NOTE:
If your students do not have a background in the subject, you might want to develop a research scramble for them. Please see the next page for a sample research scramble.

Finding the answers is so much fun. You may want the students to work in a group (2-3).

Sample
Research Scramble
(Montgomery Bus Boycott: 1955)

1. What is known historically as the Montgomery Bus Boycott of 1955?

2. In what year was Rosa Parks born?

3. What was Rosa Parks' maiden name?

4. On what date and day of the week was Rosa Parks arrested?

5. What was the Women's Political Council?

6. Who was Joann Robinson?

7. What university played a major role in the Montgomery Bus Boycott?

8. What is the name of the organization that was considered the umbrella organization for the boycott?

9. Who was chosen to be the leader of the organization?

10. On what day did the Montgomery Bus Boycott begin?

11. On what day did the Montgomery Bus Boycott end?

12. Who was the mayor of Montgomery, Alabama in 1955?

13. What are the contents of the 14th Amendment?

14. Who was Fred Gray?

15. On what day was the bus segregation on city buses in Montgomery ruled unconstitutional?

16. How many days was the Montgomery Bus Boycott of 1955?

17. The first organizational meeting for the boycott was held at what church?

18. Who was ED Nixon?

19. What is a car pool?

20. Who were the four women named in the Browder V Gayle lawsuit?

Note: The answers to the Research Scramble can be found in the Resource Section of the workbook.

Topic Brain Storm Exercise

Using some of the answers from the Research Scramble, develop three possible topics. Remember, the topic is a phrase.

Possible Topic 1

Possible Topic 2

Possible Topic 3

Step Two
Develop A Research Question and Preliminary Thesis

Develop a research question and a preliminary thesis on your topic. The research question, hypothesis, and the topic should be parallel.

Example:

- **Topic:** The topic of the research project is a phrase that gives the reader insight into what the researcher will explore. The topic must be narrow
  - **Example:** Rosa Parks' Contributions to the Montgomery Bus Boycott

- **The Research Question** is an interrogative sentence in which you want to answer. The paper's topic should be included in the research question.

- **Example:** What were Rosa Parks' contributions to the Montgomery Bus Boycott?

- **Preliminary Thesis:** The preliminary thesis provides an educated guess about your topic; it serves as the answer to your research question. The preliminary thesis should have a subject and a point of view.

Example: Rosa Parks, the mother of the Civil Rights Movement, made meaningful contributions to the Montgomery Bus Boycott of 1955.

- **NOTE:** The topic leads to a question; the question should be answered by your preliminary thesis as well as your thesis.

- **NOTE:** The topic is a phrase, the question an interrogative sentence, and the thesis a sentence with a subject and point of view.

TOPIC +
Research Question +
+Preliminary Thesis =
_____

Keys to an Organized Paper

Research Question and Preliminary Thesis Exercise

Using one of the topics from your "possible topics" list, develop a research question and a preliminary thesis. Be sure to follow the equation:

Topic +
Research Question +
Preliminary Thesis

_____

Step 3
Develop The Proposal

- After the student develops the topic, research question, and preliminary thesis, the student should draft a proposal. The research proposal is an explanation of the proposed research project. It should provide for the instructor and the student insight as to why the student desires to research the topic and provide information concerning the student's knowledge about the topic. The proposal should include the following:

  - The title of research
  - A research question.
  - A preliminary thesis for the research paper;
    - **Note:** The preliminary thesis as well as the final thesis should answer the research question.
    - **Note:** The thesis must have a subject and a point of view.
  - Why you would like to research the topic
  - How much you already know about the topic
  - A preliminary bibliography

  - **Note:** At this point in the research process, the instructor should provide direction concerning the format for the paper. The format example that will be used in this workbook is the Modern Language Association (MLA) format. See the bibliography at the end of the workbook for online guides and tutorials for the Modern Language Association format.

Proposal Exercise (One)

Develop a proposal for the topic chosen in the research question/preliminary thesis exercise.

Hint: Writing a research paper begins before you have collected the resources needed to write the rough draft. It begins when the topic is selected.

Step 4
Identify Preliminary Sources

- The preliminary sources are important. They will help the writer development the proposal and preliminary outline.

- **Suggestion:** All kinds of sources can be used for the research project: books, magazine articles, videos (*You Tube*, *TED*), CD's, and field research (go to museums), and interviews.

- Also identify the bibliographic format that will be followed.

  o Example: The Modern Language Association (MLA) format is used for literature papers.

- Great online source for the MLA format:

  http://owl.english.purdue.edu/owl/resource/747/01/

  http://content.easybib.com/citation-guides/.

Identify the MLA Format

Go to the Purdue Owl Web Site. Answer the following questions:

1. What is the bibliographic format for a book?
2. What is the bibliographic format for a source on You Tube?
3. What is the bibliographic format for an interview?

Sample Proposal

Name
Course
Date

✦ Topic: Rosa Parks' Contributions to the Montgomery Bus Boycott

1. When I was a child, my mother would often tell me the story of Rosa Parks. She said Mrs. Parks' arrest on December 1, 1955 changed the way African Americans are treated on city buses. I would like to find out more about Rosa Parks' contributions to the boycott.

2. My research question: Did Rosa Parks make meaningful contributions to the Montgomery Bus Boycott?

3. My preliminary thesis: Mrs. Parks made very meaningful contributions to the Montgomery Bus Boycott.

Note: Preliminary Sources
I have used the Modern Language Association (MLA) format for my references.

Bibliography for Preliminary Sources

King, Martin Luther, Jr. *Stride Toward Freedom*. New York: Harper and Row, 1958.

Parks, Rosa. *Rosa Parks: My Story*. New York: Puffin Books, 1992.

"Montgomery Bus Boycott." *You Tube. 5 August 2011. Web. 3 February, 2013.*

Step 5
Sample Preliminary Outline

Note: This is a topic outline. When developing a topic outline, use words and phrases.

Topic: "Rosa Parks' Contributions to The Montgomery Bus Boycott"

I. Historical Overview of the Montgomery Bus Boycott
    A. Montgomery Bus Laws
    B. Rosa Parks Arrest
    C. Thesis: Rosa Parks' Contributions

II. Rosa Parks' Contributions
    A. First Contribution
    B. Second Contribution
    C. Third Contribution

III. Conclusion

Step 6
Gathering Sources

The researcher must choose the sources for the research paper carefully. It is important to read or view the sources carefully. Be open. All kinds of sources can be used in the research paper. Below is a list of possible types of sources:

- Scholarly book
- Books from popular culture
- Biography
- Journal Article (usually a scholarly article)
- Magazine Article (usually from a popular magazine)
- Interview
- Survey
- Newspaper
- DVD
- CD
- Internet

The sources gathered for the research paper fall into two categories: primary and secondary sources.

Primary sources are original documents such as novels, plays, movies, photographs, speeches, television programs experiments, a patient's chart, the results from original research. They may include:
- Autobiographies
- Movies
- Inteviews

Secondary sources provide analysis of primary sources. This may include:
- Critical papers
- Report on a speech
- Review of a scientific findings
- An analysis of a poem

When selecting sources for a paper, examine the content closely. When evaluating an article, the researcher should:
- Examine the title. How does it relate to your topic?
- Read the author's biography. Is the author an authority on the subject?
- Read the author's notes.
- Read the opening and closing paragraphs. Is this an article that you should examine further?

Step 7
Take Notes

Taking good notes is very important. The researcher must be careful to document all sources properly. There are four types of note cards a researcher may develop: Summary Note Card, Direct Quote, Paraphrase Note Card, Researcher's Thoughts Note Card.

Type of Card	Outline Section	Card #

Author's name needed for paraphrase or quotation note card. Be sure to include a page number on the card if the quote or paraphrase comes from a printed source.

Bibliography Cards

The Bibliography card is very important in the note taking process. It is the address to your sources. If you develop a quotation card or a paraphrase card from a source, you must have a bibliography card for that source. Example: If you have five quotations from one source, you must have a bibliography representing the source. If you actually use the quotation in your paper, you can simply copy the information from your bibliography card.

Below is a Sample Bibliography Card for a Book

Author's Name
Title of Book
Place of Publication
Publisher
Date

Step 8
Develop the Final Outline

Suggestion: write a sentence outline for this step. The sentence outline is one in which the writer uses complete sentences. The sentence outline will help the writer think carefully about the thesis sentence as well as the topic sentences for the paper.

Sample Sentence Outline

Topic: "Rosa Parks' Contributions to the Montgomery Bus Boycott"

I. The Montgomery Bus Boycott is a major American Historical event.
   - A. It took place in Montgomery, Alabama.
   - B. The Boycott started on December 5, 1955.
   - C. Rosa Parks was the human catalyst for the Montgomery Bus Boycott.
   - D. Rosa Parks made two significant contributions to the Montgomery Bus Boycott of 1955.

II. One of the contributions that Rosa Parks made to the Montgomery Bus Boycott was to give all Americans a voice to speak out against inequalities.

III. The second contribution Rosa Parks made to the Montgomery Bus Boycott was to help people to understand the importance of quiet protest.

IV. My intent in this paper was to show the two important contributions Rosa Parks made to the Montgomery Bus Boycott of 1955.

Step 9
Write the Rough Draft

Six Steps to Writing A Great Rough Draft

1. Know the correct tense. Follow the tense of the format used.
2. Follow the sentence outline you have created.
3. Place your thesis statement in the introductory paragraph. Remember it must have a subject and point of view.
4. Be sure to underline the topic sentences in each one of your paragraphs. If you find it difficult to write the topic sentence, write that sentence first and make it the first sentence in each paragraph.
5. Make sure your paper has a concluding paragraph.
6. Be sure to check your references. (Note: The references serve as the addresses to the sources used in the paper.)

Step 10
Review Rough Draft

Directions: Go over the paper using the Research Paper Checklist.

RESEARCH PAPER REVISION CHECK LIST

General

1. ___ Does your paper adequately support or prove the thesis / purpose statement?

Introduction

2. ___ Have you identified your subject in the introduction?

3. ___ Have you provided any background information?

4. ___ Do you have a thesis statement with a subject and point of view?

Body

5. ___ Does the body of your paper present evidence from a wide variety of reliable sources?

6. ___ Did you restate your thesis in the conclusion of your paper?

Style and Punctuation

7. ___ Have you achieved sentence variety by using many kinds of sentences - short and long sentences; simple, compound, complex, declarative, exclamatory; and sentences that begin with difference parts of speech?

8. ___ Have you employed the correct use of punctuation?

9. ___ Have you used complete sentences throughout the paper?

Sources/Documentation

10. ___ Is there a work-cited page that lists the bibliographic sources used in the paper?

11. ___ Have you documented all quotes and paraphrases?

12. ___ Have you used the correct form of documentation for your bibliography?

Step 11
Revise and Proofread
the Rough Draft

Students should be given ample time to revise their papers.

Revising the paper gives the writer an opportunity to:

✦ Re-see!

✦ Re-think!

✦ Re-write!

Step 12
Submit the Final Draft

Cheers!

⚓ **Note:**

⚓ **Research papers can follow several formats. Two of the formats used often are Modern Language Association (MLA) and American Psychological Association (APA).**

Resources

1. Research Paper Definitions
2. Sample Resources

   a. Books and Magazines
   b. Media
   c. Other sources
   d. Pictures
3. Poem
4. Mini Conference Plan

5. Two Additional Sample Topics

Research Paper Definitions

1. **Analytical Research**– Separates issues, examines and comments on each one - then forms an opinion or comes to a conclusion.

2. **Annotations**– Brief notes that describe the contents of a book or article. The annotations go directly below the bibliography entry.

3. **Bibliography Card**-- These are cards that contain factual information - author, title, and publication facts

4. **Call Number**– A numbering system in the card catalog that classifies sources.

5. **Card Catalog**– An alphabetical list of authors, titles, and subjects to reflect the holding in the library; most library catalogs are online.

6. **Critical or Argumentative Research**– Interprets and argues an issue in order to arrive at some type of judgment.

7. **Endnotes for Documentation of Sources**– Uses the traditional superscript numerals within your paper. You will need to replace your in-text citations with superscript numbers. Your citations should then appear as double spaced entries on the "Notes" page at the end of your paper.

8. **Field Research: Research such a field trips to museum and interview.**

9. **Hypothesis**– A prediction made before reading the sources closely. This educated guess guides the search for information by focusing attention on specific aspects of a topic.

10. **Informational Research**– Gathers and summarizes facts - leads to factual results.

11. **Note Cards**– Provides material for writing the rough draft.

12. **Paraphrase Note Card**– A version of the original written in your own words in about the same length as the source.

13. **Primary Sources**– The original findings or words of a writer, whether it is a poem, novel, or cases study.

14. **Precise Note Card**– A condensed version of the original as written in your own words.

15. **Quotation Note Card**– A verbatim copy of the original material.

16. **Rough Summary**– Jotting down an idea that may or may not be used in the paper.

19. Secondary Sources– Comments and observations about the original poem, novel, case study, speech, and so on.

20. Subject– A broad subject area of study: Ex. Montgomery Bus Boycott of 1955

21. **Working Bibliography Cards**– Placed in alphabetical order, these cards serve as a guide to sources for note taking on your narrowed topic. These are cards that contain factual information - author, title, and publication facts.

2. Sample Resources

It is important for students to understand the many resources that can be used when developing the research paper. Below are samples of sources on the Montgomery Bus Boycott. Note: The bibliographic format used is the Modern Language Association Format.

1. Books and Magazines

Branch, Taylor. *Parting the Waters: America in the King Years, 1954-1963*. New York: Simon & Schuster, 1988.
Gray, Fred. *Bus Ride to Justice*. Montgomery: Black Belt Press, 1995.

King, Martin Luther, Jr. *Stride Toward Freedom*. New York: Harper and Row, 1958.

Montgomery Bus Boycott Papers. PR171. L Alabama Department of Archives and History.

Parks, Rosa. *Rosa Parks: My Story*. New York, Puffin Books, 1992.

Robinson, Joann. *The Montgomery Bus Boycott and the Women Who Started It*. Ed. David
        Garrow. Knoxville: University of Tennessee Press, 1987.

2. Internet:

Alabama Department of Archives and History.http://www.archives.alabama.gov/teacher/rights/rights1.html.
http://www.jimcrowhistory.org

3. Media

Outkast. "Rosa Parks." Aquemini. Organized Noize, 1998.

"Montgomery Bus Boycott." *You Tube*. 6 July 2013. Web. 3 February 2014.

4. Other Sources

"Using Primary Sources in the Classroom." *Civil Rights Movement Unit Lesson 1: Riding the Bus –
        Taking a Stand*. Alabama Archives and History. 8 July 2013.
        http://www.archives.alabama.gov/teacher/rights/rights1.html .

Montgomery Bus Boycott Timeline. 8 July 2013. http://students.spsu.edu/asemenov/timeline.html

381 Days: The Montgomery Bus Boycott Story. 8 July 2013. http://www.sites.si.edu/exhibitions/381.

Purdue Owl Writing Lab. 9 July 2013. http://owl.english.purdue.edu/owl/resource/747/08/

3. Pictures can be used as sources.

Pictures can be included as sources. The pictures that follow were taken from the Alabama Department of Archives site. This is the link: http://www.archives.alabama.gov/aho.html .Most states have a Department of Archives and History.

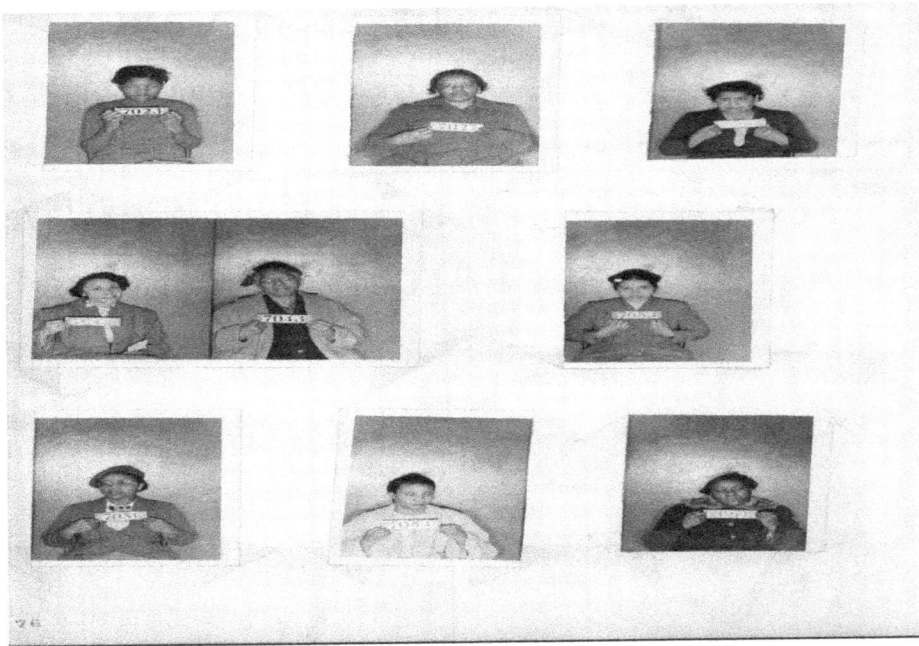

SAME AS 11939
PAGE 551

312

These pictures come from the arrest logs of the Montgomery Bus Boycott. On the next page are the signatures of those arrested. See if you can match the pictures with the names.

2-7-56 — Bay ...
2-13-56 — Bell ...
2-15-56 — Lucas ...   5-30-56

12-2-10-56	6991	Rt	Syria Turner (P)	6	29	O	15	CO	... 9	EBI
12 "	6992	Rt	Lillie Mae Quarles	6-	26	RO	18	CF	2 years prob	
1-2-12-56	6993	Rt	James A. Smith (P)	16	29	IO	18	CM	Nolle Prosqui	FBI
2-12-56	6994	Rt	Garna Croskey (P)	16	16	OM	—	CM	$100 + cost	FBI
2-13-56	6995	Rt	Obie B. Wooten	7	M	M	14	WM	4 years	FBI
15 "	6996	Rt	James C. Johnson	4	18	U 00	9	CM		
2-14-56	6997	Rt	Julius Wright (P)	6	17	RE	12	CM	2 years prob	FBI
"	6998	Rt	Norris Butler	6	31	OO	14	CM	No Bill	FBI
"	6999	Rt	Georgia Wilkerson	6	I	Tt	9	CF	Nolle Prosequi	
1-2-15-56	7000	Rt	Richard E. McLendon (P)	9	I	U II	10	WM	14 years 3-1-56	FBI
2-15-56	7001	Rt	Willie Bruce (P)	6	26	WOO	13	CO	10 years 6-6-56	FBI
"	7002	Rt	Ruth Flowers	4	30	HT 00	—	CM	2 years	FBI
"	7003	Rt	John Smith	10	32	OO	—	CM	13 months	FBI
2-11-56	7004	Rt	Oliver Smith (P)	16	I	U II	8	CM	Nolle Pros 2-17-56	FBI
"	7005		Dock May (P)	16	I	U 00	11	CM	REVERSED	
2-17-56	7006	Rt	Oranetta Richardson	I	19	M	19	CF	Life imprisonmt	FBI
"	7007	Rt	George Dewey Walker Jr.	9	26	R O	18	CM	No Bill 5-31-56	FBI
"	7008	Rt	Nathan Loveless	10	17	U 00	18	CM	2 years for QL	FBI
2-11-56	7009	Rt	Jacob James (P)	6	9	Rr	11	CO	Dia by trial CPC	FBI
2-17-56	7010	Rt	Lillie Bell Robinson (P)	6	I	a Ua	15	CF	Nolle Prosequi	
2-18-56	7011	Rt	Fred D. Gray (P)	21	27	MO	13	CM	Nolle Pros 3-24-56	FBI
"	7012	Rt	Wilson Patrick (P)	10	9	Ra	6	CO	50 + cost	FBI
2-18-56	7013	Rt	Richard Robinson (P)	7	8	U 00	15	WM		
2-20-56	7014	Rt	Tommy Gilchrist (P)	16	19	I O	14	CO	$100 + costs	FBI
" "	7015	Rt	Robert Jackson (P)	21	I	Trt	4	CM	2 yrs prob	FBI
2-21-56	7016	Rt	Clarence Gissendaner	11	I	U II	10	CM		FBI
"	7017	Rt	William McBryde	I	32	M I	—	CM	$500 + costs	
2-21-56	7018	Rt	Ralph D. Abernathy (P)	21	3		16	CM		
2-21-56	7019	Rt	Rev A.W. Hoffman (P)	21			4	CM		
"	7020	Rt	R. J. Glasco (P)	21			20	CO		
"	7021	Rt	E. D. Nixon (P)	21	13		19	CM		
"	7022		L. R. Bennett (P)	21		(3)		CM		
"	7023	Rt	Addie J. Hamerter (P)	21	32	MO	—	CF		
"	7024	Rt	Rev H. H. Hubbard (P)	21	17		17	CM		
"	7025	Rt	Walter Smith (P)	21	I	OI	6	CM		
"	7026	Rt	Rev W. J. Powell (P)	21	21	I O	13	CM		

This is the arrest logbook. Who is number 7011? What contribution did he make to the boycott?

Copy of the Leaflet Announcing the Boycott
from
The Montgomery Bus Boycott and the Women Who Started It
by Joann Robinson

This is for Monday, December 5, 1955

Another Negro woman has been arrested and thrown into jail because she refused to get up out of her seat on the bus for a white person to sit down.

It is the second time since the Claudette Colbert case that a Negro woman has been arrested for the same thing This has to be stopped.

Negroes have rights, too, for if Negroes did not ride the buses, they could not operate. Three-fourths of the riders are Negroes, yet we are arrested, or have to stand over empty seats. If we do not do something to stop these arrests, they will continue. The next time it may be you, or your daughter, or mother.

This woman's case will come up on Monday. We are, therefore, asking every Negro to stay off the buses Monday in protest of the arrest and trial. Don't ride the buses to work, to town, to school, or anywhere on Monday.

You can afford to stay out of school for one day if you have no other way to go except by bus.

You can also afford to stay out of town for one day. If you work, take a cab, or walk. But please, children and grown-ups, don't ride the bus at all on Monday. Please stay off of all buses

Text of Flyer Circulated by Montgomery Improvement Association Following Settlement of Boycott:

December 19, 1956

Integrated Bus Suggestions

This is a historic week because segregation on buses has now been declared unconstitutional. Within a few days the Supreme Court Mandate will reach Montgomery and you will be re-boarding integrated buses. This places upon us all a tremendous responsibility of maintaining, in face of what could be some unpleasantness, a calm and loving dignity befitting good citizens and members of our Race. If there is violence in word or deed it must not be our people who commit it.

For your help and convenience the following suggestions are made. Will you read, study and memorize them so that our non-violent determination may not be endangered. First, some general suggestions:

1. Not all white people are opposed to integrated buses. Accept goodwill on the part of many.

2. The whole bus is now for the use of all people. Take a vacant seat.

3. Pray for guidance and commit yourself to complete non-violence in word and action as you enter the bus.

4. Demonstrate the calm dignity of our Montgomery people in your actions.

5. In all things observe ordinary rules of courtesy and good behavior.

6. Remember that this is not a victory for Negroes alone, but for all Montgomery and the South. Do not boast! Do not brag!

7. Be quiet but friendly; proud, but not arrogant; joyous, but not boistrous.

8. Be loving enough to absorb evil and understanding enough to turn an enemy into a friend.

(Cont)   Now for some specific suggestions:

9. The bus driver is in charge of the bus and has been instructed to obey the law. Assume that he will cooperate in helping you occupy any vacant seat.

10. Do not deliberately sit by a white person, unless there is no other seat.

11. In sitting down by a person, white or colored, say "May I" or "Pardon me" as you sit. This is a common courtesy.

12. If cursed, do not curse back. If pushed, do not push back. If struck, do not strike back, but evidence love and goodwill at all times.

13. In case of an incident, talk as little as possible, and always in a quiet tone. Do not get up from your seat! Report all serious incidents to the bus driver.

14. For the first few days try to get on the bus with a friend in whose non-violence you have confidence. You can uphold one another by glance or prayer.

15. If another person is being molested, do not arise to go to his defense, but pray for the oppressor and use moral and spiritual forces to carry on the struggle for justice.

16. According to your own ability and personality, do not be afraid to experiment with new and creative techniques for achieving reconciliation and social change.

17. If you feel you cannot take it, walk for another week or two. We have confidence in our people.

GOD BLESS YOU ALL.

THE MONTGOMERY IMPROVEMENT ASSOCIATION

The Rev. M. L. King, Jr., President

The Rev. W. J. Powell, Secretary

Source: Inez Jessie Baskin Papers, Alabama Department of Archives and History, Montgomery, Alabama. URL: http://www.alabamamoments.state.al.us/sec55ps.html

Many types of sources can be used when researching a topic. I have included this poem about Rosa Parks and the Montgomery Bus Boycott as a type of literary source.

Mind Chatter: for Rosa Parks
By
Ramona L. Hyman, PhD

Her name: Rosa Parks
The day: One
The year: 1955
The month: December
The place: Montgomery, Alabama

Rosa: she tired she say
She tired when she board the bus
Walked down the center aisle-tired,
Sat (in the first of the last ten pairs of seats)
Tired.

Fable go:
> *Black folks couldn't ride up front*
> *Black folks seats in back of the bus*
> *They just like bugs*
> *Sit 'em in the back of the bus so,*
> *Tired, tired Rosa-she sit down in the back of the bus*

Bus got crowded
Driver tell black folks sitting
In the first of the last ten pairs of seats
To stand-"make it light on yourselves—stand."

Rosa ain't stand
(ain't make it light)

Fable go:
King say:
> *"Rosa Parks anchored (anchored)*
> *By accumulated indignities of*
> *daysgone by, the boundless*
> *aspirations of generations yet unborn."*

King say:
> *"Rosa Parks a victim (a victim)*
> *Of the forces of destiny."*

King say:
"When the cup of endurance runs over,
The human personality cries out."

Rosa Parks' poem (cont.)

Rosa Parks, she cry out, she cry
For the black African brought on
A slave ship-packed like sardines in stale water
She cry, she cry out so
I can sit on the bus
She cry; she get arrested
She get fingerprinted
She quiet

Fable go:
Nobody know the trouble she see
Nobody know but Jesus

Rosa Parks tired; black folks tired
She found guilty on 5 December 1955
Black folks tired; they start the boycott
Cause they tired
My mama tired, too
She in the boycott
Yo mama, yo daddy in it, too
They walk. They don't catch the bus
They crawl; they don't catch the bus
They walk. For over a year:
They go to court, keep
Going to court.

The court gets some sense

Fable go:
June 1956 Montgomery Court says:
Back of the bus sitting for black folk ain't right
November 1956 United States Supreme Court says,
Back of the bus sitting for black folk ain't right.

Rosa parks stopped walking
Black folks stopped walking
White folks stopped walking, too

Rosa Parks get some rest
Black folks get some rest
White folks-they gets some rest, too.

5. Mini Conference Plan

The mini conference is a meaningful pedagogical outcome to the theme-based research.

The Mini Conference is a one day or half day conference. The time allotted for the conference will depend on the following:

- Number of students in the classroom.
- Number of papers to be presented.
- Length and/or time allotted for the paper presentations.

The Mini Conference in Seven Steps

1. Develop a conference committee. Note: These students will help you to plan the conference.
2. Announce the conference.
3. Send out a call for papers.
   a. Ask each student to write an abstract for the paper.
4. Develop a program for the conference.
5. Decide how much time students will be give to present the paper. Example: Usually, for a class of twenty students, 10 minutes per presentation is given.
6. Encourage students to be creative. Some students, for example, may dramatize the research findings or write a poem.
7. Have fun as you learn!

Research Scramble Answers

1. What is known historically as the Montgomery Bus Boycott of 1955?
   a. The Montgomery Bus Boycott of 1955 was a 381-day boycott; the residents boycotted the segregated bus system in Montgomery, Alabama.

2. In what year was Rosa Parks born?
   a. Rosa Parks was born on February 14, 1913.

3. What was Rosa Parks' maiden name?
   a. Rosa Parks' maiden name was Mc Cauley.

4. On what date and day of the week was Rosa Parks arrested.
   a. Rosa Parks was arrested on Thursday, December 1, 1955.

5. What was the Women's Political Council?
   a. The Women's Political Council was a group of educated professors who supported and sponsored many of the Civil Rights activities in Montgomery, Alabama.

6. Who was Joann Robinson?
   a. Joann Robinson, a professor at Alabama State University in 1955, was the professor who authored the boycott leaflet.

7. What university played a major role in the Montgomery Bus Boycott?
   a. Alabama State University

8. What is the name of the organization that was considered the umbrella organization for the boycott?
   a. Montgomery Improvement Association

9. Who was chosen to be the leader of the organization?
   a. Dr. Martin Luther King, Jr.

10. On what day did the Montgomery Bus Boycott begin?
    a. December 5, 1955

11. On what day did the Montgomery Bus Boycott end?
    a. December 21, 1955

12. What is a car pool?
    a. When a group of people share rides to and from work

13. What was the name of the lawsuit used to fight bus segregation?
    a. Browder vs. Gayle

Research Paper Scramble Answers

14. Who were the four women named in the Browder V Gayle lawsuit?

    a. Claudette Colvin

    b. Ameilia Browder

    c. Susie McDonald

    d. Louise Smith

15. Who was the mayor of Montgomery, Alabama in 1955?

    a. William Tacky Gayle

16. What United States Amendment did the boycott lawyers used to fight bus segregation?

a. 14th

17. Who was Fred Gray?

    a. Lawyer for the plaintiffs

18. On what day was bus segregation on city buses in Montgomery ruled unconstitutional.

a. June 6, 1956 (Montgomery Courts); November 1956 (United States Supreme Court)

19. The first organizational meeting for the boycott was held at what church?

a. Holt Street Baptist Church

20. Who was ED Nixon?

a. In 1955 Mr. Nixon was the chair of the Montgomery Chapter of the National Association for the Advancement of Colored People.

Additional Research Paper Subjects

- Bombing of the Sixteenth Street Baptist Church in Birmingham, Alabama

- Children Who Participated in the Civil Rights Movement

- Black Churches' Contributions to The American Civil Rights Movement

- The Impact of the Civil Rights Movement on the Hip Hop Generation